# 2021
# DIARY

# DEC 2020/JANUARY 2021

**MON**
**28**

**TUE**
**29**

**WED**
**30**

**THUR**
**31**

New Year's Day

**FRI**
**1**

**SAT**
**2**

**SUN**
**3**

# JANUARY 2021

MON
4

TUE
5

WED
6

THUR
7

FRI
8

SAT
9

SUN
10

# NOTES & THOUGHTS

# JANUARY 2021

MON
## 25

---

TUE
## 26

---

WED
## 27

---

THUR
## 28

---

FRI
## 29

---

SAT
## 30

---

SUN
## 31

# NOTES & THOUGHTS

# FEBRUARY 2021

**MON**
1

**TUE**
2

**WED**
3

**THUR**
4

**FRI**
5

**SAT**
6

**SUN**
7

# FEBRUARY 2021

## MON
### 8

## TUE
### 9

## WED
### 10

## THUR
### 11

## FRI
### 12

## SAT
### 13

Valentine's Day
## SUN
### 14

# NOTES & THOUGHTS

# FEBRUARY 2021

MON
## 15

TUE
## 16

WED
## 17

THUR
## 18

FRI
## 19

SAT
## 20

SUN
## 21

# NOTES & THOUGHTS

# FEBRUARY 2021

MON
22

TUE
23

WED
24

THUR
25

FRI
26

SAT
27

SUN
28

# MARCH 2021

MON
1

TUE
2

WED
3

THUR
4

FRI
5

SAT
6

SUN
7

# MARCH 2021

MON
## 8

TUE
## 9

WED
## 10

THUR
## 11

FRI
## 12

SAT
## 13

SUN
## 14

# NOTES & THOUGHTS

# MARCH 2021

MON
15

TUE
16

WED
17

THUR
18

FRI
19

SAT
20

SUN
21

# NOTES & THOUGHTS

# MARCH 2021

MON
## 22

TUE
## 23

WED
## 24

THUR
## 25

FRI
## 26

SAT
## 27

SUN
## 28

# NOTES & THOUGHTS

# MARCH/APRIL 2021

MON
## 29

TUE
## 30

WED
## 31

THUR
## 1

FRI
## 2
Good Friday

SAT
## 3

SUN
## 4
Easter

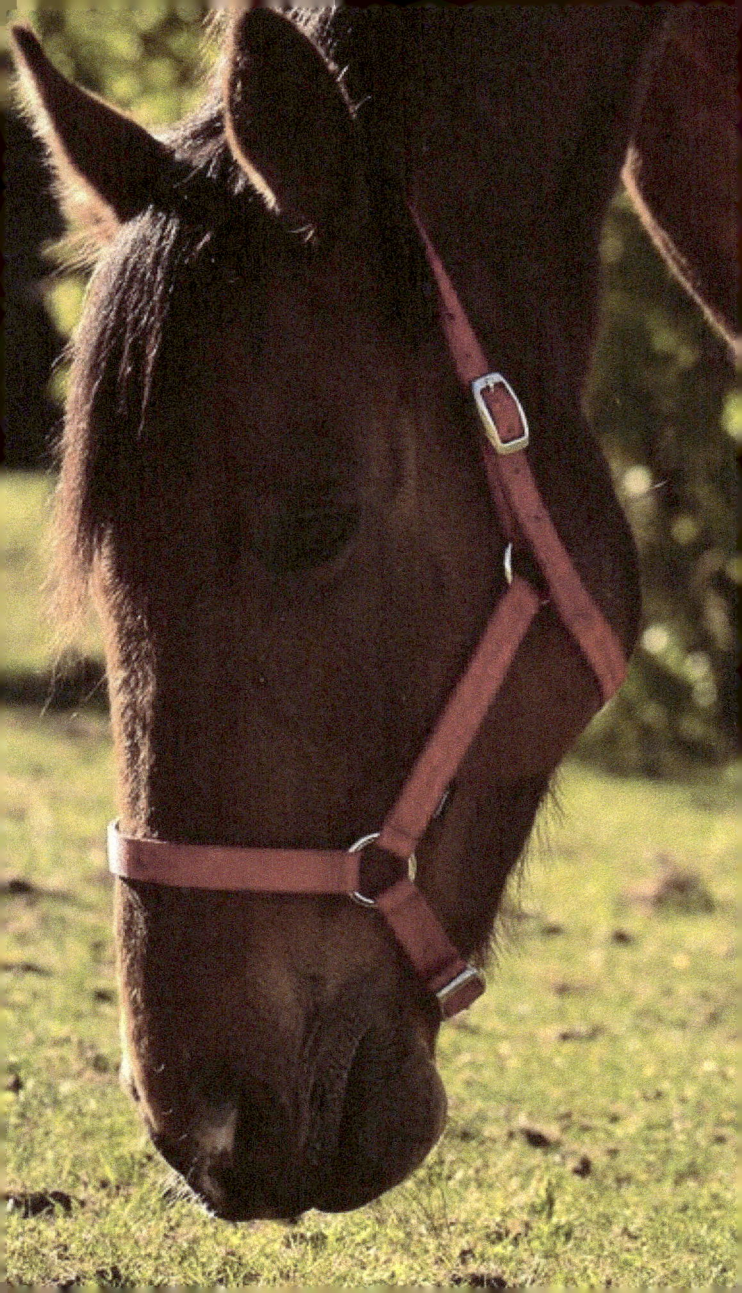

# APRIL 2021

**MON**
5

**TUE**
6

**WED**
7

**THUR**
8

**FRI**
9

**SAT**
10

**SUN**
11

# NOTES & THOUGHTS

# APRIL 2021

MON
12

TUE
13

WED
14

THUR
15

FRI
16

SAT
17

SUN
18

# NOTES & THOUGHTS

# APRIL 2021

MON
19

TUE
20

WED
21

THUR
22

FRI
23

SAT
24

SUN
25

# NOTES & THOUGHTS

# APRIL/MAY 2021

MON
26

TUE
27

WED
28

THUR
29

FRI
30

SAT
1

SUN
2

# MAY 2021

## MON
3

## TUE
4

## WED
5

## THUR
6

## FRI
7

## SAT
8

## SUN
9

Mother's Day

# NOTES & THOUGHTS

# MAY 2021

MON
10

TUE
11

WED
12

THUR
13

FRI
14

SAT
15

SUN
16

# NOTES & THOUGHTS

# MAY 2021

MON
17

TUE
18

WED
19

THUR
20

FRI
21

SAT
22

SUN
23

# NOTES & THOUGHTS

# MAY 2021

MON
24

TUE
25

WED
26

THUR
27

FRI
28

SAT
29

SUN
30

# NOTES & THOUGHTS

# MAY/JUNE 2021

Memorial Day

## MON
### 31

## TUE
### 1

## WED
### 2

## THUR
### 3

National Donut Day

## FRI
### 4

## SAT
### 5

## SUN
### 6

# JUNE 2021

MON
7

TUE
8

WED
9

THUR
10

FRI
11

SAT
12

SUN
13

# NOTES & THOUGHTS

# JUNE 2021

MON
## 14

---

TUE
## 15

---

WED
## 16

---

THUR
## 17

---

FRI
## 18

---

SAT
## 19

---

Father's Day

SUN
## 20

# NOTES & THOUGHTS

# JUNE 2021

MON
## 21

TUE
## 22

WED
## 23

THUR
## 24

FRI
## 25

SAT
## 26

SUN
## 27

# NOTES & THOUGHTS

# JUNE/JULY 2021

MON
28

TUE
29

WED
30

THUR
1

FRI
2

SAT
3

SUN
4

Independence Day

Independence Day Observed

**MON**
**5**

**TUE**
**6**

**WED**
**7**

**THUR**
**8**

**FRI**
**9**

**SAT**
**10**

**SUN**
**11**

# NOTES & THOUGHTS

# JULY 2021

MON
## 12

TUE
## 13

WED
## 14

THUR
## 15

FRI
## 16

SAT
## 17

SUN
## 18

# NOTES & THOUGHTS

# JULY 2021

MON
19

TUE
20

WED
21

THUR
22

FRI
23

SAT
24

SUN
25

# NOTES & THOUGHTS

# JULY/AUGUST 2021

MON
26

TUE
27

WED
28

THUR
29

FRI
30

SAT
31

SUN
1

# AUGUST 2021

MON
2

TUE
3

WED
4

THUR
5

FRI
6

SAT
7

SUN
8

# NOTES & THOUGHTS

# AUGUST 2021

MON
9

TUE
10

WED
11

THUR
12

FRI
13

SAT
14

SUN
15

# AUGUST 2021

MON
16

TUE
17

WED
18

THUR
19

FRI
20

SAT
21

SUN
22

# NOTES & THOUGHTS

# AUGUST 2021

MON
23

TUE
24

WED
25

THUR
26

FRI
27

SAT
28

SUN
29

# NOTES & THOUGHTS

# AUGUST/SEPTEMBER 2021

MON
30

TUE
31

WED
1

THUR
2

FRI
3

SAT
4

SUN
5

# SEPTEMBER 2021

## MON
6

## TUE
7

## WED
8

## THUR
9

## FRI
10

## SAT
11

## SUN
12

# NOTES & THOUGHTS

# SEPTEMBER 2021

MON
13

TUE
14

WED
15

THUR
16

FRI
17

SAT
18

SUN
19

# NOTES & THOUGHTS

# SEPTEMBER 2021

MON
20

TUE
21

WED
22

THUR
23

FRI
24

SAT
25

SUN
26

# NOTES & THOUGHTS

# SEPTEMBER/OCTOBER 2021

MON
27

TUE
28

WED
29

THUR
30

FRI
1

SAT
2

SUN
3

# OCTOBER 2021

## MON
4

## TUE
5

## WED
6

## THUR
7

## FRI
8

## SAT
9

## SUN
10

# NOTES & THOUGHTS

# OCTOBER 2021

MON
11

TUE
12

WED
13

THUR
14

FRI
15

SAT
16

SUN
17

# OCTOBER 2021

**MON**
18

**TUE**
19

**WED**
20

**THUR**
21

**FRI**
22

**SAT**
23

**SUN**
24

# NOTES & THOUGHTS

# OCTOBER 2021

MON
25

TUE
26

WED
27

THUR
28

FRI
29

SAT
30

Halloween

SUN
31

# NOTES & THOUGHTS

# NOVEMBER 2021

MON
1

TUE
2

WED
3

THUR
4

FRI
5

SAT
6

SUN
7

# NOVEMBER 2021

MON
## 8

TUE
## 9

WED
## 10

THUR
## 11
Veterans Day

FRI
## 12

SAT
## 13

SUN
## 14

# NOTES & THOUGHTS

# NOVEMBER 2021

MON
15

TUE
16

WED
17

THUR
18

FRI
19

SAT
20

SUN
21

# NOVEMBER 2021

MON
22

TUE
23

WED
24

THUR                          Thanksgiving Day
25

FRI
26

SAT
27

SUN
28

# NOTES & THOUGHTS

# NOVEMBER/DECEMBER 2021

MON
29

___

TUE
30

___

WED
1

___

THUR
2

___

FRI
3

___

SAT
4

___

SUN
5

# DECEMBER 2021

MON
6

TUE
7

WED
8

THUR
9

FRI
10

SAT
11

SUN
12

# NOTES & THOUGHTS

# DECEMBER 2021

MON
13

TUE
14

WED
15

THUR
16

FRI
17

SAT
18

SUN
19

# NOTES & THOUGHTS

# DECEMBER 2021

MON
20

TUE
21

WED
22

THUR
23

FRI
24

Christmas Day

SAT
25

SUN
26

# NOTES & THOUGHTS

# DECEMBER 2021

## MON
### 27

## TUE
### 28

## WED
### 29

## THUR
### 30

New Year's Eve

## FRI
### 31

## SAT

## SUN

# HOLIDAYS
## 2021

| | |
|---|---|
| JANUARY 1ST | FRIDAY - NEW YEAR'S DAY |
| JANUARY 18TH | MONDAY - MLK DAY |
| FEBRUARY 14TH | SUNDAY - VALENTINE'S DAY |
| FEBRUARY 15TH | MONDAY - PRESIDENTS DAY |
| APRIL 2ND | FRIDAY - GOOD FRIDAY |
| APRIL 4TH | SUNDAY - EASTER |
| MAY 9TH | SUNDAY - MOTHER'S DAY |
| MAY 31ST | MONDAY - MEMORIAL DAY |
| JUNE 4TH | FRIDAY - NATIONAL DONUT DAY |
| JUNE 20TH | SUNDAY - FATHER'S DAY |
| JULY 4TH | SUNDAY - INDEPENDENCE DAY |
| JULY 5TH | MONDAY - INDEPENDENCE DAY OBSERVED |
| SEPTEMBER 6TH | MONDAY - LABOR DAY |
| OCTOBER 11TH | MONDAY - COLUMBUS DAY |
| OCTOBER 31ST | SUNDAY - HALLOWEEN |
| NOVEMBER 11TH | THURSDAY - VETERANS DAY |
| NOVEMBER 25TH | THURSDAY - THANKSGIVING DAY |
| DECEMBER 25TH | SATURDAY - CHRISTMAS |

NOTES:

# CONTACTS

NAME

ADDRESS

HOME

WORK

CELL

FAX

EMAIL


NAME

ADDRESS

HOME

WORK

CELL

FAX

EMAIL


NAME

ADDRESS

HOME

WORK

CELL

FAX

EMAIL

# CONTACTS

NAME
..............................................................................

ADDRESS
..............................................................................

HOME
..............................................................................

WORK
..............................................................................

CELL
..............................................................................

FAX
..............................................................................

EMAIL
..............................................................................


NAME
..............................................................................

ADDRESS
..............................................................................

HOME
..............................................................................

WORK
..............................................................................

CELL
..............................................................................

FAX
..............................................................................

EMAIL
..............................................................................


NAME
..............................................................................

ADDRESS
..............................................................................

HOME
..............................................................................

WORK
..............................................................................

CELL
..............................................................................

FAX
..............................................................................

EMAIL
..............................................................................

# CONTACTS

NAME
......................................................................................
ADDRESS
......................................................................................
HOME
......................................................................................
WORK
......................................................................................
CELL
......................................................................................
FAX
......................................................................................
EMAIL
......................................................................................

NAME
......................................................................................
ADDRESS
......................................................................................
HOME
......................................................................................
WORK
......................................................................................
CELL
......................................................................................
FAX
......................................................................................
EMAIL
......................................................................................

NAME
......................................................................................
ADDRESS
......................................................................................
HOME
......................................................................................
WORK
......................................................................................
CELL
......................................................................................
FAX
......................................................................................
EMAIL
......................................................................................

# CONTACTS

NAME
.................................................................................

ADDRESS
.................................................................................

HOME
.................................................................................

WORK
.................................................................................

CELL
.................................................................................

FAX
.................................................................................

EMAIL
.................................................................................


NAME
.................................................................................

ADDRESS
.................................................................................

HOME
.................................................................................

WORK
.................................................................................

CELL
.................................................................................

FAX
.................................................................................

EMAIL
.................................................................................


NAME
.................................................................................

ADDRESS
.................................................................................

HOME
.................................................................................

WORK
.................................................................................

CELL
.................................................................................

FAX
.................................................................................

EMAIL
.................................................................................

# PASSWORDS

WEBSITE
...........................................................................

USERNAME
...........................................................................

PASSWORD
...........................................................................

NOTES
...........................................................................


WEBSITE
...........................................................................

USERNAME
...........................................................................

PASSWORD
...........................................................................

NOTES
...........................................................................


WEBSITE
...........................................................................

USERNAME
...........................................................................

PASSWORD
...........................................................................

NOTES
...........................................................................


WEBSITE
...........................................................................

USERNAME
...........................................................................

PASSWORD
...........................................................................

NOTES
...........................................................................

# PASSWORDS

WEBSITE

USERNAME

PASSWORD

NOTES


WEBSITE

USERNAME

PASSWORD

NOTES


WEBSITE

USERNAME

PASSWORD

NOTES


WEBSITE

USERNAME

PASSWORD

NOTES

# PASSWORDS

WEBSITE
................................................................................

USERNAME
................................................................................

PASSWORD
................................................................................

NOTES
................................................................................


WEBSITE
................................................................................

USERNAME
................................................................................

PASSWORD
................................................................................

NOTES
................................................................................


WEBSITE
................................................................................

USERNAME
................................................................................

PASSWORD
................................................................................

NOTES
................................................................................


WEBSITE
................................................................................

USERNAME
................................................................................

PASSWORD
................................................................................

NOTES
................................................................................

# PASSWORDS

WEBSITE

USERNAME

PASSWORD

NOTES


WEBSITE

USERNAME

PASSWORD

NOTES


WEBSITE

USERNAME

PASSWORD

NOTES


WEBSITE

USERNAME

PASSWORD

NOTES

# 2021

## JANUARY

| S | M | T | W | T | F | S |
|---|---|---|---|---|---|---|
|  |  |  |  |  | 1 | 2 |
| 3 | 4 | 5 | 6 | 7 | 8 | 9 |
| 10 | 11 | 12 | 13 | 14 | 15 | 16 |
| 17 | 18 | 19 | 20 | 21 | 22 | 23 |
| 24 | 25 | 26 | 27 | 28 | 29 | 30 |
| 31 |  |  |  |  |  |  |

## FEBRUARY

| S | M | T | W | T | F | S |
|---|---|---|---|---|---|---|
|  | 1 | 2 | 3 | 4 | 5 | 6 |
| 7 | 8 | 9 | 10 | 11 | 12 | 13 |
| 14 | 15 | 16 | 17 | 18 | 19 | 20 |
| 21 | 22 | 23 | 24 | 25 | 26 | 27 |
| 28 |  |  |  |  |  |  |

## MARCH

| S | M | T | W | T | F | S |
|---|---|---|---|---|---|---|
|  | 1 | 2 | 3 | 4 | 5 | 6 |
| 7 | 8 | 9 | 10 | 11 | 12 | 13 |
| 14 | 15 | 16 | 17 | 18 | 19 | 20 |
| 21 | 22 | 23 | 24 | 25 | 26 | 27 |
| 28 | 29 | 30 | 31 |  |  |  |

## APRIL

| S | M | T | W | T | F | S |
|---|---|---|---|---|---|---|
|  |  |  |  | 1 | 2 | 3 |
| 4 | 5 | 6 | 7 | 8 | 9 | 10 |
| 11 | 12 | 13 | 14 | 15 | 16 | 17 |
| 18 | 19 | 20 | 21 | 22 | 23 | 24 |
| 25 | 26 | 27 | 28 | 29 | 30 |  |

## MAY

| S | M | T | W | T | F | S |
|---|---|---|---|---|---|---|
|  |  |  |  |  |  | 1 |
| 2 | 3 | 4 | 5 | 6 | 7 | 8 |
| 9 | 10 | 11 | 12 | 13 | 14 | 15 |
| 16 | 17 | 18 | 19 | 20 | 21 | 22 |
| 23 | 24 | 25 | 26 | 27 | 28 | 29 |
| 30 | 31 |  |  |  |  |  |

## JUNE

| S | M | T | W | T | F | S |
|---|---|---|---|---|---|---|
|  |  | 1 | 2 | 3 | 4 | 5 |
| 6 | 7 | 8 | 9 | 10 | 11 | 12 |
| 13 | 14 | 15 | 16 | 17 | 18 | 19 |
| 20 | 21 | 22 | 23 | 24 | 25 | 26 |
| 27 | 28 | 29 | 30 |  |  |  |

NOTES:

# 2021

## JULY

| S | M | T | W | T | F | S |
|---|---|---|---|---|---|---|
|   |   |   |   | 1 | 2 | 3 |
| 4 | 5 | 6 | 7 | 8 | 9 | 10 |
| 11 | 12 | 13 | 14 | 15 | 16 | 17 |
| 18 | 19 | 20 | 21 | 22 | 23 | 24 |
| 25 | 26 | 27 | 28 | 29 | 30 | 31 |

## AUGUST

| S | M | T | W | T | F | S |
|---|---|---|---|---|---|---|
| 1 | 2 | 3 | 4 | 5 | 6 | 7 |
| 8 | 9 | 10 | 11 | 12 | 13 | 14 |
| 15 | 16 | 17 | 18 | 19 | 20 | 21 |
| 22 | 23 | 24 | 25 | 26 | 27 | 28 |
| 29 | 30 | 31 |   |   |   |   |

## SEPTEMBER

| S | M | T | W | T | F | S |
|---|---|---|---|---|---|---|
|   |   |   | 1 | 2 | 3 | 4 |
| 5 | 6 | 7 | 8 | 9 | 10 | 11 |
| 12 | 13 | 14 | 15 | 16 | 17 | 18 |
| 19 | 20 | 21 | 22 | 23 | 24 | 25 |
| 26 | 27 | 28 | 29 | 30 |   |   |

## OCTOBER

| S | M | T | W | T | F | S |
|---|---|---|---|---|---|---|
|   |   |   |   |   | 1 | 2 |
| 3 | 4 | 5 | 6 | 7 | 8 | 9 |
| 10 | 11 | 12 | 13 | 14 | 15 | 16 |
| 17 | 18 | 19 | 20 | 21 | 22 | 23 |
| 24 | 25 | 26 | 27 | 28 | 29 | 30 |
| 31 |   |   |   |   |   |   |

## NOVEMBER

| S | M | T | W | T | F | S |
|---|---|---|---|---|---|---|
|   | 1 | 2 | 3 | 4 | 5 | 6 |
| 7 | 8 | 9 | 10 | 11 | 12 | 13 |
| 14 | 15 | 16 | 17 | 18 | 19 | 20 |
| 21 | 22 | 23 | 24 | 25 | 26 | 27 |
| 28 | 29 | 30 |   |   |   |   |

## DECEMBER

| S | M | T | W | T | F | S |
|---|---|---|---|---|---|---|
|   |   |   | 1 | 2 | 3 | 4 |
| 5 | 6 | 7 | 8 | 9 | 10 | 11 |
| 12 | 13 | 14 | 15 | 16 | 17 | 18 |
| 19 | 20 | 21 | 22 | 23 | 24 | 25 |
| 26 | 27 | 28 | 29 | 30 |   |   |

NOTES:

# 2022

## JANUARY

| S | M | T | W | T | F | S |
|---|---|---|---|---|---|---|
|  |  |  |  |  |  | 1 |
| 2 | 3 | 4 | 5 | 6 | 7 | 8 |
| 9 | 10 | 11 | 12 | 13 | 14 | 15 |
| 16 | 17 | 18 | 19 | 20 | 21 | 22 |
| 23 | 24 | 25 | 26 | 27 | 28 | 29 |
| 30 | 31 |  |  |  |  |  |

## FEBRUARY

| S | M | T | W | T | F | S |
|---|---|---|---|---|---|---|
|  |  | 1 | 2 | 3 | 4 | 5 |
| 6 | 7 | 8 | 9 | 10 | 11 | 12 |
| 13 | 14 | 15 | 16 | 17 | 18 | 19 |
| 20 | 21 | 22 | 23 | 24 | 25 | 26 |
| 27 | 28 |  |  |  |  |  |

## MARCH

| S | M | T | W | T | F | S |
|---|---|---|---|---|---|---|
|  |  | 1 | 2 | 3 | 4 | 5 |
| 6 | 7 | 8 | 9 | 10 | 11 | 12 |
| 13 | 14 | 15 | 16 | 17 | 18 | 19 |
| 20 | 21 | 22 | 23 | 24 | 25 | 26 |
| 27 | 28 | 29 | 30 | 31 |  |  |

## APRIL

| S | M | T | W | T | F | S |
|---|---|---|---|---|---|---|
|  |  |  |  |  | 1 | 2 |
| 3 | 4 | 5 | 6 | 7 | 8 | 9 |
| 10 | 11 | 12 | 13 | 14 | 15 | 16 |
| 17 | 18 | 19 | 20 | 21 | 22 | 23 |
| 24 | 25 | 26 | 27 | 28 | 29 | 30 |

## MAY

| S | M | T | W | T | F | S |
|---|---|---|---|---|---|---|
| 1 | 2 | 3 | 4 | 5 | 6 | 7 |
| 8 | 9 | 10 | 11 | 12 | 13 | 14 |
| 15 | 16 | 17 | 18 | 19 | 20 | 21 |
| 22 | 23 | 24 | 25 | 26 | 27 | 28 |
| 29 | 30 | 31 |  |  |  |  |

## JUNE

| S | M | T | W | T | F | S |
|---|---|---|---|---|---|---|
|  |  |  | 1 | 2 | 3 | 4 |
| 5 | 6 | 7 | 8 | 9 | 10 | 11 |
| 12 | 13 | 14 | 15 | 16 | 17 | 18 |
| 19 | 20 | 21 | 22 | 23 | 24 | 25 |
| 26 | 27 | 28 | 29 | 30 |  |  |

NOTES:

# 2022

## JULY

| S | M | T | W | T | F | S |
|---|---|---|---|---|---|---|
|   |   |   |   |   | 1 | 2 |
| 3 | 4 | 5 | 6 | 7 | 8 | 9 |
| 10 | 11 | 12 | 13 | 14 | 15 | 16 |
| 17 | 18 | 19 | 20 | 21 | 22 | 23 |
| 24 | 25 | 26 | 27 | 28 | 29 | 30 |
| 31 |   |   |   |   |   |   |

## AUGUST

| S | M | T | W | T | F | S |
|---|---|---|---|---|---|---|
|   | 1 | 2 | 3 | 4 | 5 | 6 |
| 7 | 8 | 9 | 10 | 11 | 12 | 13 |
| 14 | 15 | 16 | 17 | 18 | 19 | 20 |
| 21 | 22 | 23 | 24 | 25 | 26 | 27 |
| 28 | 29 | 30 | 31 |   |   |   |

## SEPTEMBER

| S | M | T | W | T | F | S |
|---|---|---|---|---|---|---|
|   |   |   |   | 1 | 2 | 3 |
| 4 | 5 | 6 | 7 | 8 | 9 | 10 |
| 11 | 12 | 13 | 14 | 15 | 16 | 17 |
| 18 | 19 | 20 | 21 | 22 | 23 | 24 |
| 25 | 26 | 27 | 28 | 29 | 30 |   |

## OCTOBER

| S | M | T | W | T | F | S |
|---|---|---|---|---|---|---|
|   |   |   |   |   |   | 1 |
| 2 | 3 | 4 | 5 | 6 | 7 | 8 |
| 9 | 10 | 11 | 12 | 13 | 14 | 15 |
| 16 | 17 | 18 | 19 | 20 | 21 | 22 |
| 23 | 24 | 25 | 26 | 27 | 28 | 29 |
| 30 | 31 |   |   |   |   |   |

## NOVEMBER

| S | M | T | W | T | F | S |
|---|---|---|---|---|---|---|
|   |   | 1 | 2 | 3 | 4 | 5 |
| 6 | 7 | 8 | 9 | 10 | 11 | 12 |
| 13 | 14 | 15 | 16 | 17 | 18 | 19 |
| 20 | 21 | 22 | 23 | 24 | 25 | 26 |
| 27 | 28 | 29 | 30 |   |   |   |

## DECEMBER

| S | M | T | W | T | F | S |
|---|---|---|---|---|---|---|
|   |   |   |   | 1 | 2 | 3 |
| 4 | 5 | 6 | 7 | 8 | 9 | 10 |
| 11 | 12 | 13 | 14 | 15 | 16 | 17 |
| 18 | 19 | 20 | 21 | 22 | 23 | 24 |
| 25 | 26 | 27 | 28 | 29 | 30 | 31 |

NOTES: